Keep Trying!

by Martha E. H. Rustad

PEBBLE
a capstone imprint

Pebble Explore is published by Pebble, an imprint of Capstone
1710 Roe Crest Drive
North Mankato, Minnesota 56003
www.capstonepub.com

Library of Congress Cataloging-in-Publication Data
Names: Rustad, Martha E. H. (Martha Elizabeth Hillman), 1975- author.
Title: Keep trying! / Martha E. H. Rustad.
Description: North Mankato : Capstone Press, 2021. | Series: Health and
my body | Includes bibliographical references and index. | Audience:
Ages 6-8 | Audience: Grades 2-3 | Summary: "Life is full of surprises and
challenges, and it's not always fair. How you respond to those surprises
and challenges is what's important. Learn how to bounce back from
problems by taking charge of your decisions and actions" —Provided by
publisher.
Identifiers: LCCN 2020027230 (print) | LCCN 2020027231 (ebook) |
ISBN 9781977132215 (hardcover) | ISBN 9781977133212 (paperback) |
ISBN 9781977154545 (pdf)
Subjects: LCSH: Resilience (Personality trait)—Juvenile literature. |
Self-confidence—Juvenile literature. | Emotions—Juvenile literature.
Classification: LCC BF698.35.R47 R878 2021 (print) | LCC BF698.35.
R47 (ebook) | DDC 155.4/191—dc23
LC record available at https://lccn.loc.gov/2020027230
LC ebook record available at https://lccn.loc.gov/2020027231

Image Credits
Shutterstock: Brocreative, 25; courtyardpix, 24; Ekaterina Gladskikh,
18; fizkes, 11; Flamingo Images, 16, 17; imtmphoto, 4; iofoto, 21;
Monkey Business Images, 14, 26; Nirat.pix, 13; Odua Images, 9; Olena
Yakobchuk, 27; Patrick Foto, 5; photonova, design element throughout;
Riccardo Mayer, 7; Rido, cover; Samuel Borges Photography, 8; SergiyN,
29; TinnaPong, 22; wavebreakmedia, 19

Editorial Credits
Editor: Christianne Jones; Designer: Sarah Bennett; Media Researcher:
Morgan Walters; Production Specialist: Laura Manthe

All internet sites appearing in back matter were available and accurate
when this book was sent to press.

Table of Contents

Bold words are in the glossary.

What Is Resilience?

Everyone makes mistakes. Parents and siblings make mistakes. Teachers and friends make mistakes. Even you make mistakes!

After making a mistake, you may feel like giving up. You might want to quit. If you try again, that is called **resilience**. Trying again can be hard. It might seem easier to quit.

But being resilient is healthy. You can learn from a mistake. You can bounce back. Don't give up. Keep trying until you get it right. You can learn to be resilient!

Making Mistakes

When you make a mistake, it is OK to feel upset. It is OK to feel disappointed. Let your feelings happen. It is better to feel your emotions than to pretend everything is fine.

Find a way to safely **express** your feelings. You could write your feelings down. Or you could make a silly face in the mirror. You need to make yourself feel better.

Take a break. Take a few deep breaths. Come back and try again when you feel calm.

When you feel calm, take a look at what happened. Look closely at your mistake. Ask yourself questions. What worked? What didn't work? What could you do differently next time?

Then think again. Look at your mistake from another angle. Maybe there is another way.

Try again. You could change part of your **strategy**. Or you could try a new way to solve the problem.

When you try again, you might make another mistake. That is OK. It might be time for you to ask for help.

Everyone needs help sometimes. You could ask someone who knows how to solve the problem. They might have a **solution**. Or you could ask someone else who is also trying. They might have ideas for what to try next.

When you succeed, you should celebrate! Be proud of yourself. You bounced back. You are resilient!

Practicing

Practice resilience. You will get better at trying again and not giving up. Each time you practice being resilient, you learn new skills.

Try again at things you are good at. If you are good at kicking a soccer ball, practice kicking. If you are good at drawing, draw a picture.

Doing well will give you **confidence**. Then you will know that you can do hard things.

Find chances to practice resilience. You might feel **nervous**. Be brave! A good time to practice is when you are learning something new.

Jo wanted to ride her bike. She tried and fell off. Her knee really hurt. She stopped and took a deep breath. She tried again. But she fell again.

Jo wanted to give up. Instead she asked for help. Her older brother held her steady. She kept trying over and over again. Then she finally rode her bike on her own!

Another time you can practice is when you are solving a hard problem. You might feel frustrated. Keep working! Try another way of looking at the problem.

Kai's class was learning math. She thought she understood. But she kept getting wrong answers. She felt so mad!

Kai took a break. She got a drink of water. She took some deep breaths. Then she came back. Kai grouped the numbers a different way. She got the right answer!

Bad things happen to everyone. You might feel sad. You might feel mad. Resilience can help you deal with the bad things.

Raj felt really sad when his cat died. He felt mad too. He had to get his feelings out. Raj let himself cry. His dad hugged him. They felt sad together.

Raj knew he would always miss his pet. But he also knew he could ask his family for help. It helped him feel better. Raj would not be mad and sad forever.

Healthy Choices

We can't control everything in our lives. A resilient person takes charge. They control what they can. They make healthy choices.

One thing you can be in charge of is taking care of your body. Choose healthy foods. Be active. Go outside. Get regular sleep.

You need to be healthy so your body and brain can stay strong. Otherwise you might just give up when mistakes happen.

You can also control your **reaction** to change. Change is part of everyone's life. You might have a substitute teacher one day. Or maybe a friend has to cancel a play date.

Be ready for when plans change or if your usual schedule is different. Resilience helps you make a healthy choice.

You can stay calm. You know you can handle changes. Things will get better. You are ready to handle anything that happens.

Resilient people choose to help others. Knowing you can help others gives you confidence.

If a friend is struggling, you can give them a hand. They might be too embarrassed to ask for help. But you know that it is OK to ask for help. You can be their helper.

If someone is sad, you can let them know they are not alone. You know that everyone needs support from friends and family. You can give them hope.

Moving Forward

Resilient people are not afraid of making mistakes. They ask questions. They bounce back from a problem and move forward. They learn and get better every day. They can look at troubles and know that they can figure it out.

You might feel embarrassed when you make a mistake. But you know you can try again. Things will get better. You know that you are not alone. You can ask for help.

Practice being resilient every day. Don't give up, even when you want to. You are strong and smart.

When you make a mistake, you can smile. You can take a deep breath and try again. You know how to focus on finding a way to solve the problem.

A resilient person knows that there is a bright side. Even when things look hard, you can learn and grow from your challenges. Move forward and keep trying. Never give up!

Glossary

confidence (KAHN-fi-duhns)—a feeling or belief that you can succeed

express (ek-SPRESS)—to show how you feel or think by doing something

nervous (NUR-vuhss)—feeling worried

reaction (ree-AK-shuhn)—how you act when something happens to you

resilience (ri-ZIL-yuhns)—the ability to keep trying after something doesn't work out

solution (suh-LOO-shuhn)—a way to solve a problem

strategy (STRAT-uh-jee)—a plan

Read More

Bushman, Susanne M. *Don't Give Up*. Minneapolis: Jump!, 2020.

Olson, Elsie. *Be Strong!: A Hero's Guide to Being Resilient*. Minneapolis: Abdo, 2020.

Wright, Jasmyn. *I'm Gonna Push Through*. New York: Atheneum Books for Young Readers, 2020.

Internet Sites

Building Resilience
www.kidshelpline.com.au/teens/issues/building-resilience

Building Your Character: Resilience
www.healthforkids.co.uk/staying-healthy/building-your-character-resilience

Index